Readers are encouraged to go to *www.MissionPointPress.com*
to contact the author or to find information on how to buy this
book in bulk at a discounted rate.

Designed by Ali Sabbagh
Edited by Chris Kassel
Copy organizing by Kara Malack & Sara Hall
Inspired by Eider James
Photography by unsplash.com

Published by Mission Point Press
2554 Chandler Rd.
Traverse City, MI 49696
(231) 421-9513
www.MissionPointPress.com

ISBN: 978-1-954786-24-0
Library of Congress Control Number: 2021905162

Printed in the United States of America

Papa's Rules for Life

A grandfather's desire to share words of wisdom with his grandson

KEITH FAMIE

Published by Mission Point Press

Author Keith Famie has another book "Living through the Lens."
His website can be found at keithfamie.com

DEDICATION

I would like to dedicate this collection of life rules to all those little ladies and gentlemen who are on their own amazing journey. My wish is that these might help you as you sail your vessel through the many waters of life.

A heartfelt thank you to all my family, you have helped me look into my own mirror of life to better understand where I have been and always where I am going, you're my lighthouse of love guiding my way. A special shout out to my little grandson, it was you that inspired this book. YOU better read it when you get older.

I love and cherish all of you so much.

Papa Keith

INTRODUCTION

When a grandchild steps into your world and steals your heart as my grandson Eider did, you start reflecting on your own life journey and quickly realize that youth is both precious and fleeting. As you look back from the perspective of an elder, you hope you can share a bit of your own experience and wisdom in the time you have left.

This book is a collection of sincere thoughts and heartfelt advice that I would like to pass on to others as I am passing it along to Eider. Whereas my own failures in life may have outweighed my relative successes, I have always taken solace in the fact that there is a rainbow after every storm and that tough times are always followed by sunshine. I have learned that if you want to stack the deck in your favor, you will find no tool more valuable than the Golden Rule: treating others as you wish to be treated. I believe wholeheartedly in cherishing and nurturing a positive network and encouraging it to become a part of your very essence. When climbing your personal mountains, disappointments are merely the steppingstones you use to reach the next level.

I hope to instill this philosophy in Eider as he gets older, and it is my wish that this book will provide other young people the common sense required for their own success along the pathways that steer them through the wonderful journey they are about to begin.

Papa Keith

Always say please and thank you | *Why?*

A simple 'please' and 'thank you' go a long way. This act of kindness will always reflect on you positively. Do this regardless of your personal feelings for the person you are addressing.

Clean as you're cooking | *Why?*

When you're ready to eat, you will have very little left to clean up. The more you plan ahead and do ahead of time, your chances for success will be greater and you will have more enjoyment of the meal.

Try to be observant of all that is happening around you | *Why?*

First and foremost, for your own personal safety. Second, the smallest details in life often turn out to be the most significant and life-changing, both for you and for others. Size does not determine importance.

Remember a wise person is one who listens more than they speak | *Why?*

When you listen more than you speak, you will be perceived as an interested, trustworthy person. Try to offer constructive thoughts throughout the conversations but never overstate your opinion.

To be respected, you must first show respect | *Why?*

Treat others as you would like to be treated. This is known as the Golden Rule for a reason. People should not expect to be respected based solely on their accomplishments, their wealth or their looks. Instead, everyone may expect to be respected for their individuality.

Do good and good will come | *Why?*

Karma is often viewed as cosmic revenge, but I have always viewed karma as a positive force. If you structure your life around a willingness to help others, every small act of kindness you offer will be repaid. Make it a point every day to make a stranger feel good about themselves.

Never be afraid to say hello to strangers | *Why?*

Everyone has value and everyone has a story worth sharing. Others will appreciate you for your interest in their lives. I can't stress the importance of this enough: you never know where a friendly encounter will take you. The first step in many of my most interesting journeys in my life was a conversation with a stranger.

Hard work & passion for what you do is the pathway to happiness | *Why?*

When you're doing what you really enjoy for work, it won't feel like work no matter how hard it is. You will go to bed tired but satisfied, waking up the next day excited to dive right back in.

If you're doing it for the money, that's okay – but have a plan to get the job you're striving for | *Why?*

Many times in life you may have to take a job to pay bills and it may not be exactly what you want to do. Try to have a vision for where you eventually want to be, and you WILL get there.

Keep family and friends close | *Why?*

Nurture family relationships and cherish your close friends. They are by far the best investment you can make for yourself.

The network you develop in life will always reflect who you are and how people see you | *Why?*

This is essential, the people and community (a.k.a. the network) you associate with will directly reflect on who you are. Be wise to this in the social media world: what you post and who you associate with will reflect on your character.

Be okay with being wrong, often | *Why?*

Being wrong is something we all face from time to time and showing humility in the face of a mistake and admitting it is a short path to respect and learning.

Never ever forget: Manners
make the person | *Why?*

Others will always notice if you show basic manners.
Using good manners gains you respect:

Say 'excuse me' when you burp or fart, open the door for others;
especially elders, shake hands and say, "it's nice to meet you,"
keep your elbows off the table when you're eating, never talk with
food in your mouth, and remember only swear if it's necessary;
don't swear just to hear the words leave your mouth.

All the money in the world can't buy
you a second of time | *Why?*

As you get older, you will find that the most precious thing that
life has to offer you is time. Always keep the passing of time as a
focus in your life. We all take time for granted, and as I get older,
I wish I had been more in-tune with how (and with whom) I spent
my time. We only get one go-around in life and it is best to learn
the value of time while you are still young; it will serve you well
later on.

Stay humble and kind | *Why?*

Behave with humility and kindness in all your dealings and others will always enjoy being around you. Also, the vibes given off by a humble person are admired by nearly everyone and this will establish you as a natural leader.

Never burn a bridge when you leave one job for another | *Why?*

First, you never know what the future holds; you may find an opportunity right back at that job in the future. Second, the employer you're leaving now is your personal ambassador for all the time you spent working there; they can have such an impact on your life journey. (Another important reminder: always get a letter of reference from your last employer before leaving.)

You don't have to be the best. You do have to strive to be the best at what you do | *Why?*

No matter how good you are, someone else can do it better. You need to be okay with that and also learn from those who have mastered what you are trying to do. Develop a reputation for being the hardest worker who always strives for excellence, and you will find this trumps anyone who might actually be better at the job than you. In my several careers, I was not always the best at what I did, but I built a reputation of getting the job done right and not giving up until it was.

Happiness is a state of mind | *Why?*

You cannot possibly be happy all the time, no one is. Understanding that sadness is a part of our life journey is critically important. Sadness will pass, it always does. Something to keep in mind is that without difficult emotional days, we can never truly celebrate the wonderful days.

No matter how hard you may have it, there are many others who have it much harder | *Why?*

Make it a regular habit to read about those living in third-world countries or lower-income areas to see how life is for them. This will help you stay grounded. No one likes to hear someone whine about a relatively easy life. Don't be a whiner over everyday struggles, so many others have it much harder and still choose to go through life with a smile.

Always be prepared to walk in someone else's shoes | *Why?*

In order to better understand the journey that others take through life, we must always be ready to walk a mile in their shoes to see the world through their eyes. It will benefit you as well as ensure trust in the relationships you may build with these individuals.

If you can't say something nice about someone, don't say anything at all | *Why?*

Do not develop a reputation as someone known for talking about others behind their backs. Sometimes it can't be helped but be very careful to avoid making it a habit.

Learn to play an instrument | *Why?*

I have few regrets, but one of them is that I never learned to play an instrument—hopefully someday I will. Appreciating music is one thing but being able to sit down at a piano or pick up a guitar and play music makes you far more interesting as a person. The skills you develop while learning to play allows your brain to develop in areas beyond music and broadens the way you see the world.

History is not just a subject in school. Take the time to learn about history, including the history of music | *Why?*

Being curious about history will help you chart your own journey. Being curious about the history of music will introduce you to countless passionate artists. Take a deep dive into many artists, especially the following: the entire British invasion • Motown • Bob Marley • Frank Sinatra • Elle Fitzgerald • Elvis Presley • Dionne Warwick • James Brown • Tina Turner • Andrea Bocelli • Fleetwood Mac • Elton John • Bruce Springsteen • Queen • Lady Gaga • Aretha Franklin • Bob Seger • Jimmy Buffett • Garth Brooks • Neil Diamond • Tim McGraw • Prince

Be okay with failure | *Why?*

Failure is inevitable; in fact, it's imperative to your growth and shapes who you will become. Papa had far more failures than successes. Use momentary setbacks as tools to learn from and seek to develop the ability to become your own mentor.

When possible, be empathetic at all costs | *Why?*

Sympathy and empathy are often confused, so learn the difference. Sympathy is a shared feeling, usually of sorrow, pity or compassion for another person. Empathy is a more complex emotion than sympathy; it is the ability to put yourself in the place of another and understand someone else's feelings by identifying with them. This goes back to the Papa's Rule of remembering to walk a mile in someone else's shoes.

Having money does not mean you are liked | *Why?*

Some wealthy people can be kind and nice while other wealthy people are just plain mean. Money can buy you a lovely car and a big house, but it can never make you a nice person.

Be curious. Always ask questions | *Why?*

It's the best way to teach yourself about life and all of its
wonders. There is no such thing as a dumb question, EVER.
If the question pops in your head, ask it. Small children are
masters of this; they are always asking 'why' or 'how come' to
the early childhood experiences they encounter. Be curious
and ask questions no matter how old you are.

Avoid going down the gambling hole | *Why?*

As a 19-year-old chef working in Monte Carlo, the gambling capital
of Europe, I learned early on that the house always wins. It was
exciting to go to the casinos, but I was also alone in France and
spent more time in front of slot machines than I should have.
It's fun to win but you have to remember that the casino always has
the upper hand, and in the end, my new-found activity caused me
to come back home sooner than I wanted to. The moment that the
fun of gambling turns into a need to win is when you must walk
away. These days, my rule is if I ever gamble in a casino, I bring
along a set amount to play with. That's my limit and when it's gone,
it's gone. You have to be okay with knowing that your hard-earned
cash will probably disappear and that's all part of the game.

Your most important power is your ability to have an optimistic vision | *Why?*

Visualizing your ideas often turns them into reality; a visual overview is one of the most powerful tools you own. This is no different than a vision board, it just happens to be inside your head. When you can turn your vision into expectations, then you will really see the power of visualizing.

Don't listen to pessimistic critics | *Why?*

The world is filled with negative people and some of them will cross your path. Often, it's an attitude they can't help. Feel sorry for them but do not let them influence your enthusiasm for your visions; sometimes they just need to see what you see.

It is far more satisfying to give
than to receive | *Why?*

Knowing that you have brought joy to someone's life, in a
small way or a big way, is guaranteed to enhance your mental
well-being. When you see someone who clearly has less than
you and might be looking for a boost, share what you can
spare – even if it's a small amount.

Always look at nature's creatures
with fascination and respect | *Why?*

We share our planet with many amazing wild creatures and
every one of them offers a story of a unique life being lived
right in front of you. Observe and respect these creatures.

Never let yourself be the victim | *Why?*

Accept that sometimes things just don't go your way and
learn to be okay with it.

Learn to accept criticism | *Why?*

You must consider the source. If you respect the person
and know they have your best interest at heart, listen and
find a way their criticism can help you improve.
Consider it advice.

Keep an open mind to life itself | *Why?*

Look at life as an adventure. I often ended up on paths
I never expected because I peeked through doors that
opened unexpectedly.

When it comes time for dating, always treat them like princesses and princes | *Why?*

You will always want to be known as a gal who is sweet
and caring or as a guy who is a gentleman, even if you don't
date someone for a long time.

Be open minded to life mentors | *Why?*

Papa has had many wonderful mentors throughout his life who had already carved out for themselves successful careers and families. You can learn much from other viewpoints. Don't feel like you must figure everything out on your own. Learn about life from those who are further down the same road you're on now.

Must see movies | *Why?*

Movies can help you better understand history which will give you a depth of understanding that you can then share with others. While there are many more incredible and important movies, the following are my personal favorites:
Saving Private Ryan • The Green Mile • Schindler's List • Jojo Rabbit • Wizard of Oz • Pirate Radio • Good Will Hunting • Peanut Butter Falcon • It's a Beautiful Life • Indiana Jones (series) • Forest Gump • Rocky (series) • Dallas Buyers Club • Castaway • My Octopus Teacher

How you live your life today will determine how you age tomorrow | *Why?*

Your body works as a machine, but you should also think of it as a sacred temple. Be wise about what you put in your mouth because nearly everything you eat will benefit you or hurt your health and some of effects last a lifetime. As they get older, people try to dial back the aging process after they have abused their bodies for years with poor eating and exercise habits. Live today as you want to feel and look tomorrow. You can still splurge; enjoy those moments but get back on track.

To stay fit, plan to participate in an event once or twice per year | *Why?*

When you have committed to a physical event like a race or big hike in the mountains, you more than likely must train to ensure your body is ready. The focus required to train will help you stay disciplined and motivated.

When riding a bike on a path, always announce yourself | *Why?*

When riding a bike, you always want to pass a person running, walking or riding on the left and you need to announce yourself a couple times; "passing on your left," and then say, "thank you," when they move over.

Make your bed every morning | *Why?*

There are two important reasons you should do this daily: first, this habit will set you up mentally that you are ready to tackle the days' events and second, when you go to bed it is so nice to walk into your room and find a made-up bed ready to greet you.

People you should learn about | *Why?*

Many famous people have had a profound impact on the world
you are inheriting. You will hear their names mentioned in every
walk of life. There is no question learning about the roles they
played will have an impact on who you will become. The list is
long, but here are some people to get you started:
Martin Luther King • Jane Goodall • John F. Kennedy •
John Lennon • Paul McCartney • Mark Twain • Paul Bocuse •
Picasso • Barack Obama • Neil Armstrong • Steven Spielberg •
Mother Theresa • Amelia Earhart • Rosa Parks • Lucille Ball •
Muhammad Ali • Robin Williams • Bill Gates • Anne Frank •
George Patton • Naomi Parker Fraley • Vince Lombardi •
Eleanor Roosevelt • Gandhi • Walt Disney • Neil deGrasse Tyson

Carpe Diem (Latin): "Seize the Day" | *Why?*

This phrase was introduced by the Roman poet, Horace, some
2,000 years ago. The principal idea behind it is to live each day
to its fullest because our time here is limited and you never know
when your journey in life will come to an end.

Tell your mom and dad you love them often and try to avoid staying mad at them | *Why?*

Above all, a simple truth applies to every mom and dad who ever lived: they never get tired of hearing you tell them you love them. Even so, this simple act of love is often overlooked. Another more serious reason to do it is that you cannot predict what tomorrow may bring and there is no tragedy worse than losing a loved one while on bad terms. Never take your time with your parents for granted and extend this thought to your grandparents and brothers and sisters as well.

Never take others for granted | *Why?*

This can be a tough one. It's important to acknowledge those who help you through life in any way. Never fail to appreciate someone who cares for you. Just because they are more than happy to help you in any way they can, never fail to give thanks or recognition where it's due.

Don't stand for bullying | *Why?*

Bullies come in all shapes and forms; you'll start to see a pattern in how they treat others. Never be someone who finds pleasure in picking on someone. When possible, without putting yourself or others in danger, stand up for those who can't stand up for themselves. Be the one in the crowd who sees injustice towards others and speaks up.

Always pick up the dog poop | *Why?*

If you own a dog, part of the responsibility of having a pet is to pick up their poop while you're walking. Also, never, ever be cruel to your pets. They love you unconditionally and you can learn from this by showing them the same love in return.

Pain plus time equals laughter | *Why?*

I had a wonderful opportunity years ago to have lunch
with a very well-known producer/director, Gary Marshall,
in LA. Gary created some of America's most iconic family
comedy TV shows. I asked him what makes things funny.
In response, he taught me pain plus time equals laughter.
Over time, an unpleasant event can be reviewed with a new
set of eyes allowing you to laugh at what was once painful.

Take time to learn about the Civil Rights Movement | *Why?*

In order for you to navigate through your own life, you need
to understand the history of those you share the world with.
The understanding of what our fellow black brothers and
sisters endured during those complicated times is important
to you as a future community leader.

Learn the value and understanding of a paradigm shift | *Why?*

A 'paradigm shift' occurs when the usual way of thinking about or doing something is replaced by a new and different way. That being said, remember there are always two sides to every coin. This is true with life; many times, we may think and feel one way about something and then a new perspective is presented to us that changes the entire way we felt about that thing, seeing it the way someone else sees it. Mastering this can be beneficial to you when faced with a complicated argument or discussion.

If you can help it, never leave dirty dishes in the sink | *Why?*

First, if you're living with someone, no one wants to clean up after you. Second, leaving dirty dishes in the sink will attract insects and bacteria. Third, it makes it easier when you're done cooking to just enjoy the meal.

Never ask someone to do something you won't do yourself, especially an employee | *Why?*

A good leader always leads by example, it helps build respect for who you are. When I owned restaurants, on occasion I would go in and wash dishes with my team of dishwashers at the end of the night. The gesture went a long way to demonstrate teamwork and empathy for those who had the hardest and least appreciated job in the restaurant.

For continued success, patience is one of your most important life powers | *Why?*

Learning patience in life is so important on many levels. It will help you as a person knowing that sometimes you can't get exactly what you want when you want it. People will respect you for your ability to stay calm in stressful situations. From the words of Mick Jagger, Keith Richards, and the Rolling Stones, "you can't always get what you want but you can get what you need."

A sense of humor is a valuable tool | *Why?*

Laughter is the best medicine, especially when you are able
to laugh at yourself. Others will appreciate you and enjoy
being around you if you avoid being too heavy all the time.

Before you judge someone else,
first look in the mirror | *Why?*

Too often, we jump to conclusions about someone else's beliefs
or views on life. Before going down the path of judgement,
examine your own world and life. Be honest with yourself
about improvements you could make in leading your life.

Ensure your cutting board won't slide | *Why?*

When working with a cutting board in the kitchen, to keep it from sliding, always put a piece of slightly damp paper towel under the board. The real reason why? So you don't cut yourself! DUH!

Never leave kitchen knives in the sink | *Why?*

First, you don't want yourself or anyone else to reach in and cut themselves. Second, kitchen knives should be respected. That means you clean it when you're done using it, every time.

Always protect your head | *Why?*

Throughout your adventurous life, you'll only be issued
one body and your head holds in it the most important
and precious part: your brain. While your head is hard,
it does not take much to crack your skull and cause a real
issue with the way you think and act. So, always protect
your head with protective gear when you embark on any
adventure. This means WEAR A HELMET when bike
riding or rollerblading.

Learn the value multitasking | *Why?*

Multitasking refers to the ability to manage multiple
responsibilities at once. For many years, this was viewed
as unproductive, but in the fast-paced, ever-changing
world of today, multi-tasking is essential.

Learning to develop the skills to move smoothly from one
project to another is a very powerful tool. When you shift
your focus around to various projects, quite often your
subconscious will find a way to problem-solve across those
projects. I have found that making a list of projects I plan
to work on during the day helps give them the proper
attention. Learn to hone this skill, it will serve you well
all your life.

Be an early morning riser | *Why?*

There is an old saying, "the early bird catches the worm,"
and it is absolutely true. A lot happens in the early morning
hours, so create the habit of getting up early. Always rise
before 7:30am and you will find you will be able to get a lot
done before most people are even out of bed. Believe it or
not, some like to sleep in until 10am or later. By the time
these individuals get moving, they have lost half of their day.
Keep in mind this also means you must get to bed at a
reasonable hour to get at least 6 to 8 hours of sleep.

Use your time productively | *Why?*

When I look back on my life, I find that I have wasted a great
deal of time that could have been used far more productively.
Now, I have no regrets for lost time, but it has given me a
very solid understanding of how many of the people I admire
accomplished more with their time than I did. Of course,
there was plenty of time not wasted that quite possibly led
me down productive pathways. However, there are other
times when I should have pushed myself much harder, so
learn what inspires you. Work on something related to your
passion that makes you feel productive on a different level.
You never know, you might have a book inside you just
waiting for you tell the story or maybe a painting just
waiting to come alive on canvas.

Take the stairs whenever possible | *Why?*

Make it a habit to take the stairs whenever you have a choice. It gives your legs an opportunity to work your muscles and will always be better for your health than relying on an elevator. This lesson hit me hard when I had the opportunity to film with an 80-year-old neurosurgeon, Dr. Malcom Field, during a day in his life at the hospital. Dr. Field lived by this slogan: 'No smoking. No booze. No elevators.' Trust me, at 80-years-old, this mentally sharp and physically active doctor was still saving lives and working 50-60 hours every week. Truly an inspirational man, and that day (along with the slogan) has stuck with me as an essential rule for living.

Do not be on time, be early | *Why?*

When I am planning to meet with a client or a new customer, I always make it a habit to be early by a few minutes. First, it shows respect to the person with whom you are meeting. Second, it allows you to get in the right frame of mind prior to a meeting. On the other side of this coin, I have always had a great deal of admiration for my own team members who try to be early to a meeting or a planned production. No one respects a person who is always late for everything.

Develop a dynamic work ethic | *Why?*

The dictionary definition of 'work ethic' is, "a set of values centered on the importance of doing work and reflected especially in a desire or determination to work hard." Learning early-on the value of hard work and mastering a consistent approach to any task you take on will reflect on you in ways you will not realize. Others will view how you tackle problems and plan your workflow and try to imitate this simple rule for success. No matter what you are doing, big or small, always approach it with the attitude that you will do the best job you can do.

See the silver lining in complicated times | *Why?*

The dictionary definition of a 'silver lining' is, "an advantage that comes from a difficult or unpleasant situation." A long time ago, I read a statement by Albert Einstein: "In the midst of all difficulty lies opportunity." I have always kept that in the back of my mind. My own clouds have sometimes dealt me silver linings that I did not instantly recognize. After I pushed through times that seemed unbearable, I was able to see a path I would have never expected or an idea surfaces that I am now able to pursue. Opportunity is always there; you may not see it immediately but keep the faith and work hard.

Always try to be the best YOU | *Why?*

Paying attention to how we are received by others is important in life. I know some may lead their lives with the attitude, "I don't care what other people think." This is a careless and selfish way to go through life. Like it or not, you are the ambassador of your own life as well as to those who call you a loved one or friend. So, imagine what you would like others to say about you and strive to be that person.

Sit in the front row of life | *Why?*

I'll admit, I always sat in the back row in school or at least near the back. I did this to avoid being called on so I wouldn't have to participate. This never worked out for me, but it was my hope that it would. As I got older, I began to look at life as a school classroom or lecture hall and it became clear that you will get more out of life if you sit in the front row. Pay attention, ask questions and always be present.

Drug and alcohol addiction are real. Be aware | *Why?*

Habits in life can be formed for good or bad. One of the worst habits takes you down a path of overuse of alcohol or non-medicated prescribed drugs for recreation or social fun. Anyone, and I mean anyone, can stray onto this path. Be aware of the impact this can have on your life and how it can impact the people around you who care for you most. While you may feel in control, at some point, you will crash. This is just a fact. Be wise to the wicked ways through which others may try to lure you into their world of addiction. If you find yourself caught up in any form of substance abuse, know that you will always be able to envision a time in your life you were proud of. People WILL help you if you ever accidentally go down that dark path, but it takes a lot of honesty about yourself and your situation. Lastly, never judge those who are caught in a world of uncertainty that addiction brings; they are struggling with a form of escape. Try to help them anyway you can, even if they say they are fine.

Be a positive morning person | *Why?*

No one likes a morning grouch. I know sometimes people can't help it, and I get that. But if you can learn to be a positive and focused person from the moment you get up, someone who is excited about the journey immediately ahead, you will have set yourself up to a good start. An added benefit is that others will appreciate and respect you for this outlook, especially if you're a leader.

Strive to be the unifier | *Why?*

A unifier is someone or something that brings others together.
Now, as a leader in any situation it's important to bring people
together through vision and passion. This intense, focused energy
will almost certainly create an environment for success. You must
find the confidence in yourself to believe strongly that your way is
the best way for the given situation and pass that confidence onto
others. Keep in mind that quite often, this process takes time and
patience. Not everyone will see your vision, or they may have a
natural, pessimistic attitude and that's okay, too. When those
team members come around, they can become the most effective
team players that will ensure the outcome you've strived for.

Be a team player | *Why?*

Your character while interacting with others will be scrutinized.
Having a reputation as a team player is such a powerful indicator
of who you are. Simple things like washing the dishes in the sink
(even if they are not yours) or helping someone at work even if it
takes time away from your own project reflects on your character.
If you're able to help them do it, it will pay dividends all along
your long journey through life.

Learn to ask the big questions in life | *Why?*

Who am I? What is my role here? What is my relationship with
mother nature and the world? These questions have been asked by
just about anyone who walked the planet. Everyone will ask these
questions but not all will ask them early enough in their life. Old
age is no time to be asking the big questions. Learn to ask these
questions in your youth and you may find that the search for the
answers will become your guiding compass on life's adventures.

Hit your problems head-on | *Why?*

We all face speed bumps along the road of life, and some may
turn into full-on roadblocks. Problems are inevitable. It is how
you handle issues that will define your character. Develop a plan
to recognize problems as soon as they arise, then take action.

Lean into discomfort | *Why?*

This will always lead to personal growth. When you're struggling to meet your goals, whether it is running a race or finishing a project, the journey to success is almost always met with difficulties – it is just a law of nature. How you get through the work at hand will help you better understand who you are and how well you rise to a challenge. Just relax and do the work.

Celebrate small wins | *Why?*

Confidence building is the sum total of many small accomplishments; each success adds up to give you the ability to visualize anything you tackle. These small wins will teach your brain that you can try anything, even if you fail (and you will), the small wins will keep your spirits positive.

Be a storyteller | *Why?*

Learning to tell a story is one of the most powerful tools you can develop. When you share personal stories about life experiences your audience will gain a new sense of who you are. It will also build a level of trust from others because they will be able to relate to your life's journey or have empathy for some part of the story. No matter if the story is funny, sad, or just fascinating, being able to share a story will serve you very well.

Be a collector | *Why?*

Collecting worldly treasures from the paths we have taken through life helps us remember where we have been. As we get older, it is so fun to be able to share these journeys with others. It doesn't matter what it is: a rock from a hiking trip (boy, do I have plenty of those!) or a piece of art like a small painting you bought on the streets of Paris.

Learn about the Holocaust | *Why?*

This was one of the most tragic chapters of history. It was unimaginable on all levels. Take time to go back in time and educate yourself about what it was and why it took place. You will be greatly respected for this.

Develop a love for reading | *Why?*

There is no question that a person who develops the habit of reading for enjoyment will always have a more in-depth understanding of the human condition. Explore fiction and non-fiction equally; step into the world through true life adventures of explorers who, against all odds, chose to boldly push forward on their quest. For real fun, try to get your hands on some old 'Life' magazines and step back in time through those pages to see where their focus was throughout history.

Before going to bed, make a list
for the next day | *Why?*

As a little boy, I watched my father write in a pocket-sized
notebook every night, and when I was old enough to read
and understand what it was, I looked through it. I found
very detailed notes you would expect from a WWII Airforce
Lieutenant who became an engineer in civilian life. Since my
late teens, I have been handwriting next day 'to-do' lists on a
yellow notepad every night before bed. This allows me to set
intentions for the next day and enables a more restful night
sleep because my mind can relax, and I can visualize how the
following day will go. It is always my goal to check off what I
accomplished and then start this process all over again.
It's a very healthy routine to adapt early on and one that should
stay with you for life.

Always remember that everything in life has a beginning and an end | *Why?*

As your life goes on, you will lose pets, friends, and yes, even family members. This is part of life and there is a cycle for all creatures, big and small. You will face this reality more than you want to, but always remember that the sadness that goes with losing a loved one is part of your humanity. Everyone, including me, has had to say goodbye to people we love. Grief must be embraced and acknowledged in order to move on. Those you keep in your heart will always be with you; celebrate who they were and why they were special to you. Share their story with those who knew them. You will be okay; this deep sadness will pass in time, I promise you.

Avoid appearing to be arrogant | *Why?*

To be arrogant is, "to exaggerate one's own worth or importance, often by an overbearing manner; someone who is full of self-worth or self-importance and who tells and shows that they have a feeling of superiority over others." Not many opinions are universal, but you can bet that very few people who present themselves as arrogant are well-liked.

Work to develop a confidence about yourself | *Why?*

A person who displays confidence is popular and respected and is frequently sought out for leadership roles. Confident people believe in their own abilities and are certain that positive things will happen. This trait must be honed over time from your own successes and failures. A perfect example of self-confidence can be seen in an Olympic medalist who seems to perform without fear. In fact, they have practiced their moves so many times they believe with all their hearts that they will pull it off. It's a characteristic also seen in surgeons, who have to be able to think quickly and make life and death decisions as a routine part of the job.

Have an open mind to religion and spirituality | *Why?*

We all move through life to the beat of a drum, but every person may hear a different drummer. Both religion and spirituality should have a place in your life. Here is the difference: Religion is a community of like-minded people who share a system of beliefs and practices. There are over 4,000 religions in the world, and most are confident that they have solved the biggest questions we all have: who are we and where are we going. A life of adventure has taught me to have an open mind, and to respect the beliefs of others, and above all, to approach these various religions with curiosity. Spirituality, on the other hand, is more how an individual gains a sense of peace and purpose. You can certainly be spiritual without adhering to any one religion and you can just as easily (and regrettably) be religious without having a trace of spirituality. The most important thing to remember as you navigate these complicated waters is the Golden Rule. Treat others as you would like them to treat you and you will have mastered all that is important in either religion or spirituality.

Do not spend yourself into debt | *Why?*

An important part of growing up is learning to manage your
money. You will find that it is very easy to spend money you don't
actually have by using credit cards. Unless you are careful, you can
quickly bury yourself in debt and digging your way out can be very
complicated. Understand the value of good credit and the
convenience of credit cards but always try to pay off debt
as often as possible. If you get into trouble, ask those around
you who have your interests at heart for advice because a fresh
perspective can be just what you need before it's too late.

Invest into your financial future | *Why?*

I wish I learned much earlier that saving a portion of every dollar
you earn adds up to a much easier retirement. You may think it
is too early to start thinking about this stage of life, but it is never
too early to develop solid financial habits. You don't have the
expenses now that will plague you later so you should be able to
create a bank savings where you can put away some of your weekly
earnings, perhaps as much as 50%. When you are older, you can
then move this into a structured financial portfolio that you can
watch grow over the years.

Once in a while, doing nothing is okay | *Why?*

I am the first to admit to being a Type A personality, making it hard for me to simply sit still and do nothing. But being able to relax and treat yourself to a period of time where you do absolutely nothing is actually healthy for your brain. It does no good to guilt yourself into thinking you always need to be productive. It has taken me almost 60 years of life to take the time to sit still and relax knowing that everything I am working on will still be there at the end of the day.

Learn to trust your intuition | *Why?*

Intuition is the ability to instantly read a situation without the need for conscious reasoning, it is a feeling in your gut that something is either right or wrong. Learning to listen to this 'inner voice' is a vital tool that will help steer you through times of indecisiveness. Another way to steer through a confusing situation is to envision someone you respect and admire being in the same place as you are and ask yourself, 'what would they do?'

Take care of your teeth | *Why?*

They are only teeth you have, of course. A good general rule is
to pay as much attention to oral hygiene as any other part of
your body since gum issues can lead to teeth problems and teeth
problems can lead to gum issues. Both have proven links to more
serious health issues. Take your dental care seriously, brush your
teeth at least twice a day, floss, use a water pik weekly and add
a good mouthwash to your routine.

Learn to be an adventurous eater | *Why?*

The world is filled with many wonderful foods, styles of cooking
and unique flavors. In order to appreciate the gastronomical
experiences available to you, you must be open-minded to new
cooking styles and unfamiliar ingredients. Your taste buds will
evolve, and you will remember these new flavors. Ask questions to
understand the origin of what you're eating and the methods of
preparation. Besides the personal satisfaction these experiences
will bring you, it will also help you become well-versed in the
culinary world and perceived by others as knowledgeable.

One rule I always lived by when visiting other countries was to
visit the markets and shops where local communities went to buy
fresh food. This is one of the best ways to learn about the culture,
so years ago I wrote a book that drives home this thought:
"You Really Haven't Been There until You've Eaten the food."

Plant a garden | *Why?*

I was never a great gardener but even without a 'green thumb,' I learned how to grow vegetables and herbs. Take the time to learn the basics about growing the items you use in your recipes. Few things you can do are more gratifying than placing a seed into the soil and watching it become a ready-to-eat menu item.

Learn to cook | *Why?*

I believe everyone should know how to prepare a healthy meal for themselves and their loved ones. Cooking may seem intimidating, but unlike brain surgery, the basics are easily mastered. All it takes is discipline and a passion for a delicious meal. You don't have to be a restaurant chef to develop confidence in the kitchen. Watch the Food Channel, read a few food magazines, and take note of what others like to cook at home. This will be a win/win for you and your entire network of loved ones and will add depth to who you are.

Learn to love mushrooms | *Why?*

There are over 50,000 species of mushroom living on earth,
many containing important nutrients that our bodies need.
There are about twenty types of fungi that we humans eat on
a regular basis. Besides the diverse flavors and textures they
bring to our menu creations, they also have a dramatic impact
on our health. When you eat mushrooms, you are helping your
gut's bacteria create a healthy inner ecosystem. A diet rich in
mushrooms boosts our immune systems and the powerful
antioxidants they provide will help lower inflammation,
a source of many health issues. Mushrooms are filled with
vitamin D and selenium, which protect your body's cells.
Vitamin D is important for muscle and bone health and
promotes growth. Learning to appreciate the vast array of
edible mushrooms will help not only your health but will
add to the adventure of cooking, something you can carry
with you for the rest of your life.

Learn to nose breathe | *Why?*

I learned about nose-breathing late in life. It seems funny to talk about something we do all day every day; taking a breath every three seconds (50,000 times a day), inhaling in roughly 30 pounds of air. So why concern ourselves with breathing? First, most of us are mouth-breathers and that ultimately has a negative effect on health. Your nose is a filter designed to strain out many particles and pollutants that would do harm to your body. Your nose, in fact, is your body's first line of defense. Learning to breathe correctly is not a new ideal, it dates back to ancient civilizations. In India, breathing was understood to bring 'Prana,' the life force, or vital energy. In China, breath is 'Chi.' Both cultures share the belief that a focus on breathing leads to clear-thinking and helps balance our minds and moods. Today, breathing techniques are incorporated in many daily rituals, from the structure of Buddhist mantras to the Catholic 'Ave Maria,' African and Native American prayers are often based on relaxation and controlled breathing. Even elite athletes who depend on a high level of cardio have built routines around breathing exercises in order to excel at their chosen sport.

Relax and do the work | *Why?*

Many years ago, while in the gym lifting weights, I would often
lose focus. A good friend made this statement: "Relax and do the
work." I have used that saying countless times over the years,
especially when competing in events. When you say to yourself,
"relax and do the work," your focus shifts to your breathing.
I find that the work then becomes easier and I can go for longer
periods of time without stopping or slowing down. This really
works great when running or long-distance biking.

Develop a healthy eating style
that works for you | *Why?*

Learning the value of healthy eating from an early age will
become one of the most important tools in your life chest.
In the 60's and 70's (when I was growing up), my parents
did not understand the value of nutritional eating habits. I
had to teach myself the lessons of what healthy eating is all
about. I now realize how helpful these lessons would have
been at a younger age and I am trying to make up for it now.
You, being young, have an incredible opportunity to impact
how your body grows and develops. Let organic fresh fruits
and vegetables become your best friends. Avoid fast food and
processed food at all costs and if you ever splurge, get back on
a healthy eating plan as soon as possible. Also, never go to bed
with a full stomach, try to eat your last meal or snack no later
than seven or eight o'clock at the latest. I am a great believer
in a wholesome breakfast; mine generally consists
of oatmeal, fresh berries, and sometimes eggs.

You need to create your own happiness | *Why?*

It's easy to blame others for the reason you are not happy, but you must always be the captain of your own vessel. It is your responsibility to find happiness in your days; it is not up to others to bring you joy. You'll find, of course, that some days are easier than others, and folks who are not in your direct network or community can and will affect how your day unfolds. Taking personal moments throughout the day to remind yourself that you alone control your moods can be extremely empowering. Never allow negative events or people to control your state of mind. A good question to ask yourself first thing in the morning is, "What is my path to happiness today?"

Learn to be diplomatic | *Why?*

Diplomacy is part of dealing with people in a sensitive and effective way. In your everyday life, you will experience a wide range of social interactions with family, friends, and in the working world. You must learn early to look for a win/win in every scenario where there is a dispute, and you have to be able to articulate it. It often helps others understand what you see and feel. Being diplomatic means being calm, not combative; it makes you the person who is looked to in order to settle issues and bring two sides together. Having grown up in a household where my parents argued daily, I found myself having to bring diplomacy to the situations more times than I wished. However, this helped me develop the skills necessary to succeed as an adult. Practice diplomacy among those closest to you and I promise it will make the times where diplomacy is needed in business and relationships that much easier.

You need to attend funerals | *Why?*

There will be times in your life when you are expected to attend funerals. They can be uncomfortable at best and at worst, they will be an overwhelming emotional experience, especially if the death is a loved one, like a mom, dad, brother, sister, or grandparent. Although funerals will be defining occasions in your life, there is no easy way to approach them. What you are feeling is grief, one of the truest and most painful emotions a person can experience. The good news is that grief lessens with time and you should realize that everyone who has ever lived has experienced loss. Death is a part of life and it is important to find ways to celebrate the memories of the person you have lost; reflect on what they stood for, talk about the funny moments you shared. Saying goodbye is never easy but by becoming an ambassador for who they were in life is probably the best way of keeping them alive in our hearts.

Try to understand divorce | *Why?*

In your lifetime, you will have friends whose parents go through a divorce. In fact, you may be one of them yourself and it may be that you feel your entire life has been turned upside down. Divorce means that mom and dad are not able to live together for one reason or another. The most important thing for you to know is that it is not your fault and you must never blame yourself. Divorce is complicated and extremely hard on everyone involved. It happens in the best of families so even if you feel like you are alone, I promise you that you are not. Everyone involved in a divorce needs time to heal and not everyone can move beyond hurt feelings at the same rate as others. Often as time passes, moms and dads find a way back to some level of friendship; it may take many months or even years, but it can happen. You will always be the bridge between mom and dad, and you can be the one who brings a level of diplomacy to the situation. I went through a divorce when my children were very young, and I am now very close to their mother. She is close to my new wife and I am good friends with her new husband. The bottom line is this: if you find yourself in the middle of a divorce, try to take a step back and know that in time everything will work out.

Embrace dinner time with family | *Why?*

We are all so busy with our work, school and afterschool
activities that it's sometimes hard to keep up with other family
members. One of the best places to check in with each other
is at the dinner table. To promote eating together as often as
possible, be a participant in the preparation and cleanup at
mealtimes. Learn to cherish stress-free conversation about the
days' happenings and laugh at funny moments while discussing
the difficult ones; these days, that means not looking at your
phone every five minutes. You are a member of a tribe and the
ritual of breaking bread together will become one of your most
cherished family moments, one that you will remember fondly
after you grow up.

Consider playing two different types of sports in school | *Why?*

Being a part of your school's athletic program will not only enhance your personal confidence level but will give you a feeling of community spirit. Never worry that you might not be as good as or as talented as others on your team. I was a terrible athlete who finally found my niche in tennis. Through a lot of practice, often alone, hitting tennis balls against the wall at a local college, I became good enough to hold my own. There are two types of sports you can participate in, one being team sports with the objective of working together to score points. Throughout your life you will find yourself part of a collection of people with a common goal, this is the simplest definition of a team. The other type of sport is a solo sport, like tennis or many track and field events, where it's you against the world. Overcoming problems alone has much to offer in terms of individual problem solving and solutions worked out in your head. Independent thinkers are often able to face complicated challenges and as Rocky would say, "Find the eye of the tiger within." Go out there and give it a shot, remembering that you don't have to be the best at your sport – you only must be the best you can be.

If you say you're going to do something, do it | *Why?*

Far more than thoughts, character is defined by actions. People will regard you by how well you follow-up with promises. No matter how big it is or how small it is, if you say you're going to do something, do it – or at the very least, attempt to do it. This can be as simple as taking out the trash or doing chores around the house or it may be something full of complexities like trying out for a team or completing a task your employer has set before you. Either way, simply saying out loud, "I'm going to do it" sets in motion the wheels of action.

Develop your superpowers of niceness | *Why?*

We can all be superheroes in the eyes of others. Of course, I am not suggesting you wear red tights and a cape, but life is hard for everyone at some point and when you go out of your way to be genuinely nice to others, especially to strangers, you have displayed a remarkable superpower known as empathy. Make all your gestures kind, always offer a helping hand and form a habit of being someone that anyone can turn to if they are in trouble. Do this and I promise you, life will reward you many times over.

Be very careful around fire | *Why?*

We rely on fire for many important things, including cooking and keeping warm but let's be clear that as an energy source, it is as dangerous as it is helpful. You and your friends should never play with fire and if you should accidentally catch something on fire, tell someone immediately. The last thing you want to do is walk away thinking it will go out on its own because it won't.

If you find yourself in a hole, just stop digging | *Why?*

Throughout your life, you will probably find yourself in a hole that you somehow managed to dig yourself. I certainly have. There's an old cowboy saying that you can rely on as a solution and even if it sounds easier said than done, it is often a remarkably simple way to avoid getting in any deeper: "just stop digging."

Don't text and drive | *Why?*

Someday you will learn to drive a car and among the many safety lessons you will have to master, this one is very important: never text while in the driver's seat. It only takes a second for an accident to occur that can change your life and the lives of those around you forever.

Working for free can be a good thing | *Why?*

From time to time, you may be asked to work for free, whether as an apprentice or an intern. In my younger days, I worked many long hours without pay in order to learn the tools of my trade. Many times my friends would tell me I was crazy for working hard for no money but I saw it differently; I saw it as an opportunity to learn from masters of the craft. You may find, like I did, that when you recognize the value of the education before the paycheck you will be more inspired by what you learn.

Work like you own the business | *Why?*

Most employees take a different approach to work than the business owner. As an owner, when all decisions are made by you, you tend to work harder and with a greater level of concern and urgency to the daily happenings. Part of successful entrepreneurship is learning to problem solve on the fly and use creative thinking to find new ways of helping the business, but you will also find that it is lonely at the top. When working for others, always try to learn the complexities of the business and show that you care as much about it as the owner and the executive management team does. This has two benefits: your employer will look at you in a more positive light and it will develop the sort of work ethic you will need if one day you choose to run your own business.

Become inspired by others | *Why?*

Throughout my life I have looked for inspiration from others to become the best 'me' I can be. I regularly seek out stories of those who have shown incredible stamina in the face of unimaginable challenges. I highly advise you find such stories among those around you, watching how others overcome struggles will help you when you look in the mirror of your own life. One of my favorite examples is the father/son team of Dick and Rick Hoyt who competed together in numerous marathons and Ironman Triathlons. Rick (the son) has cerebral palsy and during competitions his father Dick would pull him in a special boat as they would swim, carry him in a special seat in the front of a bicycle and push him in a special wheelchair as they ran; both are in the Ironman Hall of Fame.

Open doors for anyone | *Why?*

Here is the deal my little buddies: if you make it a habit to open the door for anyone who arrives there at the same time as you and say, "no, you go ahead; have a nice day," you will not only make the day of a stranger, but you will feel good about yourself. It's the simple gestures to others that mean so much.

Breathe through anxiety | *Why?*

There are times when we all encounter situations and this is
a simple fix that works wonders: sit or stand quietly and take
five deep breaths, pause, then take another five deep breaths.
The issue you are dealing with will not vanish, but I promise
you that your ability to think through the problem will be
much improved.

Scams and deception: do not trust ANYONE online | *Why?*

At one time or another we have all been approached by
someone pretending to be someone or something they
are not. Online or on the phone, this type of scam is very
common. As you start to explore the big wide world of the
internet you will no doubt encounter people who are offering
to sell you something or buy something from you, or in some
case, simply wanting to be your friend. Please (and I say
this very loudly), ask the people you trust (preferably your
parents or older brothers and sisters) to look over the profile
of who you are dealing with and offer their opinion.

Understand jealousy and harness it | *Why?*

Jealousy is a feeling of resentment, bitterness or hostility toward someone because they have something that you don't and it's something that we all experience along life's journey. Learn to turn feelings of jealousy into inspiration; become motivated to take a negative emotion and make it positive by improving yourself in whatever area is causing you to be jealous of others. As a simple example, if you are jealous of someone on your team who is more skilled than you, work at becoming better at that skill. This will help you be the best 'you' you can be.

No spitting | *Why?*

This one is simple enough. Spitting for the sake of spitting is poor manners. If some condition makes you need to spit, do it in private.

Say excuse me when in conversation | *Why?*

No one likes to be interrupted but there are times when you will need to interject something in the middle of a conversation. At such times, always say, 'excuse me,' and announce your reason for the interruption, whether you have a question or need help with a specific point being made. You will have announced yourself in two ways: first, as someone who is paying attention to the details of what is being said, and secondly, as someone with manners.

Take care of our animals | *Why?*

As a young person today, you have a genuine ability to impact the health of the planet and as the next generation of leaders, you must learn your place in the world and develop respect and wonder at the lives of other creatures. Learn that killing should not be the main focus of hunting; hunting should be reserved for procuring food. There is much to learn from our planet and much of it has been captured in nature shows. Watch them as often as you can and learn about the living world around us.

Be okay with being alone | *Why?*

Spending time by yourself is very healthy and you will find that it offers an opportunity to recharge your emotional batteries. Some people dislike being alone for extended periods, but we all encounter times where this is necessary. The key to being comfortable alone is self-confidence; if you like yourself, being alone is simply being in the company of someone you respect.

Become a critical thinker | *Why?*

Critical thinking means that you can evaluate a situation from two perspectives, inside and out. It's an ability to see both the positives and negatives of an issue and most importantly, the judgement to know what course of action is best. It's a skill that takes years to develop, but if you begin to apply it to your everyday life when young, you'll be far ahead of this old guy, for sure.

Remember it ain't over till it's over | *Why?*

t happens to friends, it happens in relationships, and it even
happens in the careers of professional athletes – they throw in the
owel (meaning, they give up) when they feel they have lost the
ability to compete. Always keep this saying in your head, "it ain't
over till it's over, and only I decide when it's over." One constant
we've all seen over the years is that those who fight through
difficulties, even when it seems that they have been beaten,
sometimes come out on top. Keep fighting for what you believe
n and once you've given your all and choose to be finished,
that's okay too, but make it your decision.

Never lose your imagination | *Why?*

Imagination is one of the special gifts we have as human beings.
The ability to conjure up an image in our brains and bring it to
life in some way may be as basic as role playing with your siblings
or creating a film as masterful as Star Wars, E.T., or the Harry
Potter series. All of these situations involved someone, adults
and children, envisioning something in their minds and bringing
it to life.

When in restaurants tip well | *Why?*

The word 'tip' dates back to 17th century England and is an abbreviation for, 'to ensure prompt service.' It used to be given to the server before a meal, and today, it is left to the server when the bill is paid. Wait staff work hard and they are generally paid less than minimum wage, so always tip them as generously as you can; I always leave 20 - 25% of the total bill.

It's ok to cry | *Why?*

Not only is it okay to cry, but it's also healthy to cry. To small children, crying comes easy; however, too often as you get older, you have been taught to hide your emotions. If you feel the need to cry and are in an environment where this is safe, go ahead, you will always feel better afterward. It is a very powerful emotion, so keep focused on the reason you are so sad so that in the end, you can move forward with a positive new direction.

Win like you're used to it | *Why?*

The world seems to be comprised of two types of winners: those who boast about a win and those who are humble and maintain an attitude that winning is something that comes naturally to them. This does not mean you can't be proud of your accomplishments, but you don't want to be seen as the kind of person who brags about them.

Learn the power of laughter | *Why?*

Laughter is among the most powerful of human emotions and it can have a tremendous effect on your sense of well-being. The best kind of laughter is the kind that makes your belly hurt and should be embraced whenever appropriate. Just remember that laughing at someone who is being picked on or hurt is never okay.

Play hard and often | *Why?*

Whether you are an adult or a child, play time is as important as work time. Nearly every successful person you read about have one thing in common: they were driven to compete, and this meant they played hard, whether as weekend athletes or individuals who ran marathons as a hobby. I'm sure they would all agree that playing competitively helps develop leadership skills.

Learn to play golf | *Why?*

I am not a golfer, not even close. However, I wish that when I was young someone had taught me the basics so I could have become at least respectable at the sport. Golf is a thinking person's sport that requires discipline and concentration in order to excel; not only that, it offers a lifetime of opportunities to bond with friends and business associates.

Be ok with how you look | *Why?*

There is only one 'you' and that is a wonderful thing. Look in
the mirror; everything you see today will change and grow.
Your genetics will impact many of these changes, but so will
how you live your life, including the amount of exercise you get,
the food you eat and so on. You may not like the way you look
now but there are some things you can change. As a young boy
and teenager, I struggled with my weight and I was picked on in
school every day. As time went on, I grew out of the person I was
and developed into a new person. The same thing will happen
to you, so be okay with who you are today. You're a one of kind
and we all love you for it.

Be a great speller | *Why?*

Okay, so anyone who knows me is laughing really hard right now
since I am the world's worst speller; but truthfully, I really admire
those who can spell. Take your time to learn a new word every
day. Understand its meaning and memorize how it is spelled.

Send personal notes | *Why?*

The day of writing personal notes seems to have passed.
Today, we rely on texting and emails and other forms of
electronic sharing. However, that also means that when
you take the time to write a note by hand, it carries with its
special meaning. Receiving a hand written note is evidence
that whoever is writing you wanted to add a personal touch,
and that is a sign of both respect and affection. Get in the
habit of sending handwritten notes and you can take it
further to custom make the stationery on which the note
is written; whoever receives the note will be touched and
impressed.

No littering | *Why?*

Littering is against the law and the fines are steep, but
more than that, it isn't right to desecrate nature in this
way. Plastic waste is especially dangerous to wildlife, so
all garbage should be put in the appropriate container.

Respect our first responders | *Why?*

Police, firefighters, sheriffs and emergency workers will affect your life many times as you grow up. We count on them to protect us or help us if we are hurt. Always treat them with respect and never be afraid of them.

Be an active part of your tribe | *Why?*

If you have a close-knit family that lives and thrives together, this is your tribe. Be aware that having a tribe you can call your own is a privilege and that some kids are not so lucky. You need to cherish and respect all family members, even knowing that you won't always agree on everything. Take pride in knowing your place within your tribe and always be a supportive member by helping out with chores, both inside and outside the house. Nobody likes mowing the lawn or vacuuming but these are household jobs that need to be done and your tribe (mom and dad, especially) should be able to rely on your help. When you are asked to chip in, do so with pride, knowing that you are a vital and irreplaceable member of your tribe and there is nothing cooler than that.

Be a self-starter | *Why?*

In any job you have, it's always better to be early than late and if you should arrive before your co-workers, see if you can begin work on any project that has been planned. Taking the initiative is a quality of a self-starter; it is a valuable habit to develop early and one that will demonstrate to your employer that you are a strong team player who does not need constant direction.

Beware of downed electrical wires | *Why?*

If ever you see an overhead electrical wire on the ground, stay away from it. You don't know if the wire is still connected to something that is sending an electric current through it. If you touch a downed wire that is still 'alive' you will receive the worst electrical shock of your life. If your friends are around, be the smart one in the group and call the police while keeping everyone away from the downed wire.

Look for landmarks when hiking | *Why?*

One life lesson that will serve you again and again is an ability to navigate through your surroundings with a basic sense of direction. When you head out on an adventure, whether it's hiking, biking, or boating on a large body of water, be the one who scans the area and finds landmarks. This might be a tall building, a certain type of tree or a rock formation—anything that will help you find your way back to the place where you set off. Once you find your landmark, decide which direction it faces. Knowing north, south, east and west is very important; remember that the sun sets in the west and rises in the east... today, tomorrow, and every day. Once you figure out which direction your object faces, head the opposite direction to return. So, if the big rock faces north, you'd head south on the way back. If you're by a river and start your adventure heading downstream, you would simply head upriver to return. Learn to create a visual map in your head by learning which direction your front porch faces and which direction the back of your house faces, then, both sides of your house. You will quickly master the art of always knowing where you are, and you should strive to be the one in any group who can instantly be relied upon to supply this information. If you do get lost on an adventure, and everyone does sometimes, don't panic, take your time to access where you came from. If you can, get to higher ground so you can see better. Of course, if you have a cell phone, never leave for an outing without making sure your phone is charged. Happy safe adventures!

Lose yourself in art | *Why?*

I am so far from being an artist, but I have always been
fascinated by one's ability to express themselves in such
a wonderful way. Expression of art in all its mediums
can enable you to transcend yourself, whether it be some
of the historical creations of the early painters such as
Rembrandt, Erté, Toulouse, Picasso, Van Gogh, Dali, Frida
Kahlo or more modern creators, even those murals you see
on sides of buildings in urban city areas. All of these offer
a unique perspective of what the artist was trying to say.
Make it a habit to go to museums whenever possible and
really let yourself go as you take time to appreciate this
type of very personal expression.

Learn and practice the value of being grateful | *Why?*

I was in my forties before I really understood this. I can tell you when and where I was at the very moment that I made the decision to start learning to have deeper gratitude for who I was and with whom I shared my life. First, let's better understand what gratitude is: it's our ability to see the good in our lives. We must learn to acknowledge the gifts that have been given to us by others and to understand how influential various people have been in our lives. A really helpful practice is to keep a notebook you can write in at the end of each day, listing the things you are grateful for. It may sound silly, but I have been doing this for many years, and it really works. Studies have proved that keeping a journal has a positive effect on your physical and mental well-being and is equally beneficial to your relationship with others.

My moment of enlightenment came while I was sitting bedside with my father, who I was caring for due to his Alzheimer's disease. He was just hours away from passing on and it was a terribly upsetting moment. For the first time, I thought back on my life and acknowledged how selfish I had been so many times. Then, when my mother passed on a few years later, I was again reminded of the importance of gratitude and the ability to express it every day, with every sunrise and every sunset. If you take nothing else away from this collection of advice, take this: nothing in life will be as important as your respect for those who help you become the person you are, and to them, you owe thanks.

Everyone has a story of how they spent their time during the COVID shutdown.

I had the wonderful pleasure of hanging with
my grandson and often the neighbors' kids
going on adventures.

Keith, Liam, Leo, Eider and Luke.

BIOGRAPHY

KEITH FAMIE
DIRECTOR /
PRODUCER

irector/Producer, Keith Famie was, for many years, known as a celebrity chef and a metro Detroit restaurateur. Famie was also a finalist on the 2001 reality television series, "Survivor: The Australian Outback." Keith hosted his own Food Network series, "Keith Famie's Adventures," traveling the world, documenting cooking styles from the plains of Africa to monk monasteries of Taiwan, to the lifestyle of Key West.

In 2004, the Adventure Chef embarked on a new journey – documentary filmmaking, saying "I didn't want to be the 'Adventure Chef' guy anymore. I wanted to help people tell their stories." Since that life-changing decision, Famie has been awarded eleven Michigan Emmys and has been nominated several other times for his rich, human-interest storytelling, from ethnic documentaries to military tribute films – never shying away from tackling difficult subject matter in his documentaries; rather, the reverse. Famie takes a subject that most seek to avoid and embraces it, approaching it from many different perspectives and weaving together the complexities of each subject. He and

his team at Visionalist Entertainment Productions create informative, entertaining films that touch a wide audience.

Since 2013, Keith has been producing and directing impactful documentaries for PBS as well as national film festivals. The subjects span topics including the military, aging, cancer, dementia, blindness, Down syndrome, and the Holocaust. In 2019, Keith published a book, *Living Through the Lens*. Through the storytelling of Keith and his team, they have been able to touch thousands of lives of those who otherwise might not have been able to share their stories.

Over the years, Keith has been actively involved in several well-respected, Michigan-based 501 (c)(3) organizations that support everything from children with cancer and hunger relief to veterans' issues.

In 2003, Keith finished the 25th anniversary Ironman Triathlon World Championship in Kona with the Team In Training for the Leukemia & Lymphoma Society. In 2015, he was awarded the 2015 Diamond Award by the Association for Women in Communications Detroit Chapter. In 2017, Keith was presented the Media Award by Gilda's Club Metro Detroit. To learn more about Keith, go to www.keithfamie.com or check out Visionalist Entertainment Productions.

Lightning Source UK Ltd.
Milton Keynes UK
UKHW020330040521
383055UK00008B/497